JENNIFER SYJUD

iPhone for Seniors 2024

A Step-by-Step Pocket Guide

First edition

This book was professionally typeset on Reedsy.
Find out more at reedsy.com

In a world where technology moves swiftly, the voyage of discovery lies not in seeking new landscapes, but in having new eyes. This book is dedicated to all the seniors who dare to see the world anew through the lens of technology. May your journey be filled with wonder and empowerment.

-Marcel Proust

Contents

1

Introduction

Welcome to "iPhone For Seniors 2024: A Step-by-Step Pocket Guide"! My name is Jennifer Syjud, and I couldn't be more excited to guide you through this thrilling journey into the world of iPhone technology. Initially, I found smartphones, especially iPhones, to be quite daunting. However, with a bit of help and dedication, I quickly became proficient, unlocking a vibrant world of innovation and convenience at my fingertips. This realm of endless possibilities, however, can sometimes seem out of reach for our senior community, which is precisely why this book came to life.

Inspired by my 94-year-old Grandma, a proud and enthusiastic iPhone user, this guide is a testament to the idea that age is but a number when it comes to embracing technology. I aim to empower seniors everywhere to not just learn but to revel in the use of their iPhones, much like my Grandma does.

In this compact guide, written simply, you'll find everything you need to become proficient with your iPhone. I've refined the vast information into a concise, easy-to-follow manual. From the initial setup to navigating the interface, mastering apps, and safeguarding your privacy and security, this book is your trusted companion. Whether you're taking your first steps into the smartphone world or transitioning to an iPhone from another device, my goal is to ensure your journey is smooth and deeply rewarding.

We'll start with the basics, ensuring you're comfortable with the physical aspects of your iPhone, like understanding its buttons and navigating the touchscreen. Gradually, we'll progress to more advanced features, ensuring you have a solid foundation before moving on. Each chapter is structured to build on the previous one, allowing you to progress at your own pace.

In addition to technical skills, this guide emphasizes the importance of online safety and privacy, teaching you how to secure your personal information and avoid common pitfalls. Digital well-being is also a key focus, ensuring that your iPhone enhances your life without becoming overwhelming.

Remember, this journey is about exploration and enjoyment. There's no rush, and every step forward is an achievement. With patience, curiosity, and this pocket guide in hand, you'll soon find yourself a confident iPhone user, ready to explore all that this incredible technology has to offer.

So let's turn the page and take the first step together into the wonderful world of iPhone for Seniors. Your adventure awaits!

2

Setting Up Your New iPhone

Welcome to the first step of your iPhone journey! This chapter is designed to help you become familiar with your iPhone in the most straightforward way possible. We'll cover the basics, from turning your iPhone on to understanding its main features like Face ID. Let's take this step by step, ensuring you feel comfortable and confident as you begin.

Turning On Your iPhone

- **Power Button:** Locate the power button on the side of your iPhone. It's the only button on the right side (for most models).
- **Turning On:** Press and hold the power button for a few seconds until the Apple logo appears on the screen. This means your iPhone is starting up.
- **Welcome Screen:** Once your iPhone turns on, you'll see a "Hello" or "Welcome" screen. Swipe up from the bottom (or press the home button on models that have one) to start the setup process.

The Home Screen

The Home Screen is your starting point. It's where all your apps are displayed.

- **App Icons:** These are little squares with pictures that represent different applications (apps) on your iPhone, like the Phone app, Messages, and Mail.
- **Dock:** At the bottom of the Home Screen, there's a row called the Dock. The apps in the Dock stay the same as you swipe between Home Screen pages, making them easily accessible.
- **Swipe to Explore:** Swipe left or right with your finger to navigate through different pages of apps.
- Basic Gestures
- **Tap:** Touching an app icon once opens the app.
- Swipe: Moving your finger across the screen lets you switch between screens or scroll through lists.
- **Pinch and Zoom:** Place two fingers on the screen and move them apart or together to zoom in or out on photos, web pages, and maps.

The Control Center

- **Accessing:** Swipe down from the top-right corner of the screen to open the Control Center. This gives you quick access to useful settings like airplane mode, Wi-Fi, and brightness.
- **Using Controls:** Tap on an icon to turn a feature on or off. You can also adjust the sliders for brightness and volume to your preference.

Charging Your iPhone

- **Charging Port:** Find the charging port at the bottom of your iPhone.
- **Plugging In:** Insert the charger into the port and connect the other end to a power outlet. A battery icon on the screen will show that your iPhone is charging.

Continuing from where we left off, let's delve into setting up Face ID and connecting your iPhone X or newer model to Wi-Fi. Both are essential steps to making the most out of your device, ensuring security and connectivity.

Setting Up Face ID

Face ID allows you to unlock your iPhone, authenticate purchases, and log in to apps simply by looking at your device.

Here's how to set it up:

- **Go to Settings:** On your iPhone, find and tap the "Settings" icon on your Home Screen.
- **Face ID & Passcode:** Scroll down and select "Face ID & Passcode." You might be asked to enter your passcode.
- **Set Up Face ID:** Tap "Set Up Face ID." Ensure you're in a well-lit area and your iPhone is held at arm's length, approximately 10-20 inches away from your face.
- **Position Your Face:** Follow the on-screen instructions. Look straight into your iPhone and position your face inside the frame. Slowly move your head to complete the circle. If you're unable to move your head, tap "Accessibility Options."
- **Complete the Scan:** After the first scan is complete, tap "Continue" and repeat the head movement for a second scan.
- **Face ID is Set Up:** Once both scans are complete, tap "Done." Your

Face ID is now set up and ready to use.

Connecting to Wi-Fi

Staying connected is crucial for downloading apps, browsing the internet, and receiving emails.

Here's how to connect your iPhone to a Wi-Fi network:

- **Open Settings:** Tap the "Settings" icon on your Home Screen.
- **Wi-Fi Settings:** Tap "Wi-Fi" near the top of the settings list. Make sure the Wi-Fi switch is toggled on; it will be green when enabled.
- **Select a Network:** Your iPhone will automatically search for available Wi-Fi networks. Find and tap the name of the network you want to join. If it's a public Wi-Fi network, it might connect automatically without a password. For private networks, you'll need the password.
- **Enter the Password:** If prompted, enter the Wi-Fi network password. This is usually set by the person or organization that set up the network. Tap "Join" after entering the password.
- **Connected:** Once connected, you'll see a checkmark next to the network name, and the Wi-Fi icon will appear in the top right corner of your screen, indicating a successful connection.

Remember, if you're using a public Wi-Fi network, be cautious about the information you share or access due to security concerns. It's generally safer to use networks that are password-protected, especially for sensitive activities like online banking.

By setting up Face ID and connecting to Wi-Fi, you're enhancing both the security and functionality of your iPhone. Face ID ensures that only you can access your device and personal data, while a Wi-Fi connection opens up a world of online activities, from browsing the web to downloading new apps and staying in touch with loved ones.

This chapter is just the beginning, meant to ease you into the world of your iPhone. Take your time to explore and get comfortable with these basics. Remember, practice makes perfect, and there's no rush. In the next chapters, we'll dive deeper into more features and functionalities. For now, celebrate your progress—you're on your way to becoming an iPhone expert!

3

Mastering Basic Navigation

Navigating your iPhone with ease is the key to enjoying all its features. This chapter is dedicated to helping you master basic navigation gestures and use Siri, your voice-activated assistant. We'll cover how to return to the Home screen, switch between apps, access the Control Center, and use Siri for various tasks like making calls and sending messages.

Basic Navigation Gestures

Understanding these simple gestures will help you move around your iPhone smoothly:

- **Swiping Up to Go Home:** Without a physical Home button, returning to the Home Screen on your iPhone X or newer is as simple as swiping up from the bottom edge of the screen. This gesture works in any app, bringing you back to your familiar Home Screen.
- **Switching Between Apps:** To see recently used apps, swipe up from the bottom edge and pause in the middle of the screen. You'll see app cards that you can swipe through. Tap on any app to switch to it. To close an app, simply swipe its card upwards.

- **Accessing the Control Center:** Swipe down from the top-right corner of your screen to open the Control Center. This is where you can quickly adjust settings like Wi-Fi, Bluetooth, screen brightness, and volume. Tap outside of the Control Center or swipe up to close it.

Using Siri for Voice Commands

Siri is your built-in assistant that can perform tasks using voice commands.

Here's how to make the most out of Siri:

- **Activating Siri:** To activate Siri, press and hold the side button on your iPhone until you see the Siri interface appear. On some models, you can also say "Hey Siri" to start a voice command session, provided you've enabled "Listen for 'Hey Siri'" in the Siri & Search settings.
- **Making Calls with Siri:** Simply tell Siri whom you'd like to call by saying something like, "Call [contact name]." If the contact has more than one number, Siri might ask you to specify which one, such as "home" or "mobile."
- **Sending Messages with Siri:** To send a message, say "Send a message to [contact name] saying [your message]." Siri will type out your message and confirm with you before sending it. If you need to make changes, just tell Siri what you want to be corrected.
- **More Siri Commands:** Siri can do much more than make calls and send messages. You can ask for the weather, set reminders, play music, and even get directions. Try commands like "What's the weather today?" or "Remind me to call John at 4 PM."

Remember, Siri is designed to understand natural language, so you don't need to memorize specific commands. Just speak as if you're talking to a person, and Siri will do its best to understand and assist you.

4

iPhone Communication Essentials

Staying connected with family and friends is one of the most rewarding aspects of your iPhone. This chapter will guide you through the essentials of communication, including making phone calls, sending text messages, and enjoying video calls with FaceTime. Let's explore these features step by step, ensuring you're comfortable reaching out to your loved ones.

Making Phone Calls Using the Phone App

The Phone app is your gateway to making and receiving calls.

Here's how to use it:

- **Opening the Phone App:** Tap the green Phone icon on your Home Screen or Dock to open the app.
- **Making a Call:** Once the app is open, you have a few options:
- **Keypad:** Tap "Keypad" at the bottom to dial a number manually. Enter the number and tap the green phone icon to start the call.
- **Contacts:** Tap "Contacts" at the bottom to see a list of people you know. Tap a contact's name, then tap the phone icon next to their

number to call them.
- **Recents:** Tap "Recents" to view a list of recent calls. Tap any name or number in the list to call them back.
- **Ending a Call:** To hang up, tap the red phone icon on the screen.

Sending Text Messages with the Messages App

Text messaging allows you to send brief messages and photos.

Here's how to use the Messages app:

- **Opening the Messages App:** Tap the green Messages icon on your Home Screen.
- **Starting a New Message:** Tap the compose button (pencil and paper icon) in the upper right corner. Enter the contact's name or phone number in the "To:" field.
- **Composing Your Message:** Tap the text field that says "iMessage" and type your message. You can also tap the camera icon to add a photo or video.
- **Sending the Message:** Tap the upward-pointing arrow to send your message. If the arrow is blue, your message will be sent as an iMessage (over the internet). If it's green, it will be sent as a standard text message.

Using FaceTime for Video Calls

FaceTime allows you to make video calls, making conversations more personal by seeing each other face-to-face.

- **Opening FaceTime:** Tap the green FaceTime icon on your Home Screen.
- **Making a Video Call:** In the FaceTime app, tap the plus sign (+) in the upper right corner. Enter the contact's name, phone number, or

email address. Tap "Video" to start a video call.

- **During the Call:** You can switch the camera view from front to back by tapping the camera icon with arrows. To mute your microphone, tap the microphone icon.
- **Ending the Call:** Tap the red phone icon to end the call.
- Remember, FaceTime video calls require an internet connection and can only be made to another Apple device, such as an iPhone, iPad, or Mac.

5

Personalizing Your iPhone Experience

Making your iPhone truly yours is not just about adding your contacts and apps; it's also about adjusting settings and organizing your Home Screen to suit your preferences and needs. This chapter will guide you through personalizing your iPhone, including adjusting display settings and organizing apps.

Adjusting Display Settings

Making your iPhone easier to read and interact with can enhance your overall experience.

Here's how to adjust some key display settings:

- **Brightness:** Control the screen brightness to make viewing comfortable in different lighting conditions. Go to Settings > Display & Brightness. Use the slider to adjust the brightness or turn on "Auto-Brightness" to let your iPhone adjust automatically.
- **Text Size:** Increase the size of the text for better visibility. Go to Settings > Display & Brightness > Text Size. Drag the slider to adjust the text size.

- **Ringtone Volume:** Adjust the volume of your ringtone so you can hear incoming calls. Go to Settings > Sounds & Haptics. Use the "Ringer and Alerts" slider to set the volume.

Organizing Apps on the Home Screen

Keeping your apps organized can help you find what you need more quickly.

- **Moving Apps:** Press and hold an app icon until all icons start jiggling. Drag the app to a new location, then tap "Done" (or press the Home button on models with one).
- **Creating Folders:** To group similar apps, drag one app onto another while in jiggle mode. This creates a folder. You can tap the folder's name to rename it. Press "Done" to finish.
- **Using the App Library:** Swipe left on your Home Screen to the last page to find the App Library, where your apps are automatically organized into categories. You can find and open apps here without cluttering your Home Screen.

6

Capturing Moments with the Camera

Your iPhone is not just a communication device; it's also a powerful camera capable of capturing life's precious moments. This chapter will guide you through taking photos and videos and managing them in the Photos app. Whether you're photographing a family gathering or capturing the beauty of nature, your iPhone makes it easy and enjoyable.

Taking Photos with the Camera App

The Camera app is your gateway to photography.

Here's how to use it:

- **Opening the Camera:** Tap the Camera app icon on your Home Screen, or swipe left from the Lock Screen to quickly access the camera.
- **Taking a Photo:** With the Camera app open, you'll see the image from the camera on your screen. Aim your iPhone at what you want to photograph. Tap the large white button at the bottom (shutter button) to take a photo.
- **Using Zoom:** Pinch the screen to zoom in or out before taking a

photo. This helps you get the framing just right.

· **Switching Cameras:** Tap the circular arrow icon to switch between the front (selfie) and rear cameras.

Recording Videos

Capturing videos is just as straightforward.

· **Switch to Video Mode:** In the Camera app, swipe right or left on the screen until you see "Video" highlighted at the bottom.
· **Start Recording:** Tap the red button to start recording a video. While recording, this button will turn into a square.
· **Stop Recording:** Tap the square button when you're finished recording.

Viewing, Organizing, and Sharing Photos

The Photos app is where all your images and videos are stored.

· **Opening the Photos App:** Tap the Photos icon on your Home Screen to view your captured moments.
· **Viewing Photos:** Your photos are automatically organized into "Years," "Months," "Days," and "All Photos." Tap on any photo to view it in full screen. Swipe left or right to browse through your photos.
· **Creating Albums:** To organize your photos, you can create albums. Go to "Albums," tap the plus sign (+), and select "New Album." Give it a name and add the photos you wish.
· **Sharing Photos:** To share a photo, view it full screen, then tap the share button (a square with an arrow pointing up). You can choose to send it via Messages, Mail, or share it on social media. Select the

contact or app you want to share with and follow the prompts.

Capturing and sharing moments with your iPhone is a wonderful way to keep memories alive and share them with loved ones. Don't hesitate to experiment with taking photos and videos, and explore different subjects and settings. With practice, you'll find more joy in capturing the beauty and wonder of the world around you.

7

Exploring the World of Apps

Your iPhone is a gateway to a vast world of apps that can entertain, inform, and simplify daily tasks. This chapter will guide you through finding and installing new apps from the App Store and highlight some essential apps that are particularly useful for seniors.

Finding and Installing Apps from the App Store

The App Store is the place to discover and download apps.

Here's how to use it:

- **Opening the App Store:** Tap the blue App Store icon on your Home Screen.
- **Browsing for Apps:** Once in the App Store, you can browse featured apps, search for specific apps, or explore categories. The "Today" tab showcases new and noteworthy apps.
- **Searching for an App:** Tap the "Search" tab in the bottom right corner, then type the name of the app or a keyword in the search bar. Tap "Search" on your keyboard.

- **Downloading an App:** When you find an app you like, tap on it to see more details. If it's free, you'll see "Get" next to the app; if it's paid, you'll see the price. Tap "Get" or the price, then confirm with Face ID, Touch ID, or your Apple ID password to install.
- **Opening Your New App:** Once the app is downloaded, you'll find it on your Home Screen or in the App Library. Tap it to open and start exploring.

Essential Apps for Seniors

Here are some app categories and examples that can be particularly beneficial for seniors:

- **Health and Fitness:** Apps like "MyFitnessPal" and "Apple Health" help you track your physical activity, diet, and even medical records, encouraging a healthy lifestyle.
- **Communication:** Besides the built-in Phone and Messages apps, consider "WhatsApp" for messaging and "Skype" or "Zoom" for video calls, making it easy to stay in touch with family and friends.
- **Hobbies and Learning:** Explore apps related to your interests, such as "Audible" for audiobooks, "Duolingo" for learning new languages, or "YouTube" for a wide range of instructional videos.
- **News and Weather:** Stay informed with apps like "The Weather Channel" for weather forecasts and "Flipboard" or "BBC News" for the latest news and articles tailored to your interests.
- **Utilities and Tools:** Apps like "Magnifying Glass + Flashlight" can be handy for reading small print, and "Find My iPhone" can help you locate your device if it's misplaced.

Exploring the App Store can be an enjoyable adventure, revealing apps that cater to your needs and interests. Remember, the best apps for you are the ones that make your life easier, more enjoyable, and more connected. Take your time to explore and don't hesitate to ask family or friends for app recommendations. With millions of apps at your fingertips, there's something for everyone.

8

Internet, Browsing, and Email

T he Internet opens up a world of information, entertainment, and communication. This chapter will walk you through connecting to the internet, browsing the web with Safari, and setting up your email accounts on your iPhone. These steps will help you stay informed, connected, and engaged with the world around you.

Connecting to the Internet

Your iPhone can connect to the Internet through Wi-Fi or cellular data.

- **Wi-Fi Connection:** To connect to a Wi-Fi network, go to Settings > Wi-Fi. Ensure Wi-Fi is turned on, then select a network from the list. If prompted, enter the password for the network and tap "Join."
- **Cellular Data:** If you're not connected to Wi-Fi, you can use cellular data to access the internet. Go to Settings > Cellular, and make sure Cellular Data is turned on. Note that using cellular data may incur charges, depending on your service plan.

Browsing with Safari

Safari is the web browser on your iPhone, designed for exploring the internet.

- **Opening Safari**: Tap the Safari icon (it looks like a compass) on your Home Screen.
- **Visiting a Website:** In Safari, tap the address bar at the top, type in a web address (like www.google.com) or a search term, then tap "Go" on the keyboard.
- **Navigating Web Pages:** Tap links to explore different pages. Swipe up or down to scroll through a page. To go back to a previous page, tap the back arrow in the bottom left corner.
- **Bookmarking a Site:** To save a website for easy access later, tap the share button (a square with an arrow pointing up), then tap "Add Bookmark." You can find your bookmarks by tapping the book icon at the bottom.

Setting Up and Managing Email Accounts

Staying in touch via email is essential.

Here's how to set up an email account:

- **Adding an Email Account:** Go to Settings > Mail > Accounts > Add Account. Select your email provider (like Google, Yahoo, or Outlook) and follow the prompts to log in with your email address and password.
- **Using the Mail App:** Once your account is added, open the Mail app from your Home Screen. You'll see your inbox with all your emails. Tap an email to read it.
- **Sending an Email:** To compose a new email, tap the compose button (a square with a pencil) in the bottom right corner. Enter the recipient's email address, a subject, and your message. Tap "Send" when you're ready.

- **Managing Emails:** You can reply to, forward, or delete emails using the options at the bottom when viewing an email. To organize your inbox, you can also move emails to different folders.

Connecting to the internet, browsing with Safari, and managing your emails are fundamental skills that enhance your iPhone experience. Take your time to explore these features, and don't hesitate to refer back to these steps whenever you need them. The internet and email connect you to a vast network of information and people, making them invaluable tools in your daily life.

9

Entertainment and Leisure

Your iPhone is not only a tool for communication and tasks but also a wonderful source of entertainment and leisure. Whether you enjoy listening to music, reading books, or staying up-to-date with the news, your iPhone brings these pleasures to your fingertips. This chapter will guide you through enjoying various media on your iPhone and how to find apps that cater to your hobbies and interests.

Enjoying Music

Your iPhone makes it easy to listen to your favorite music, whether it's songs you've purchased or streaming through music apps.

- **Apple Music:** The built-in Music app gives you access to your music library and Apple Music, where you can stream millions of songs, find new music, and listen to curated playlists. Tap the Music icon, explore the app, and play any song or playlist you like. If you're new to Apple Music, you might need to sign up for a subscription.
- **Other Music Apps:** If you prefer, you can download other music streaming apps from the App Store, such as Spotify or Pandora. These apps also offer vast libraries of music and personalized

playlists.

Reading Books and News

Your iPhone can be your portable library and newsstand, perfect for reading at home or on the go.

- **Books App:** The Apple Books app allows you to browse, purchase, and read books and audiobooks. Tap the Books icon, explore the Bookstore or your Library, and choose a book to start reading or listening to.
- **News Apps:** Stay informed with the latest news by using the Apple News app or downloading other news apps from the App Store like CNN, BBC News, or flipboard. These apps provide current events, articles, and stories tailored to your interests.

Apps for Hobbies and Interests

Whether you're into gardening, painting, cooking, or photography, there's likely an app to match your hobby.

- **Finding Hobby Apps:** Open the App Store and use the search feature to find apps related to your hobby. Type in keywords like "gardening," "watercolor painting," "recipes," or "photo editing" to find apps that interest you.
- **Exploring and Downloading:** Browse through the search results, read the app descriptions, and look at the user ratings to help you decide which apps to try. Tap "Get" to download an app, and then open it to start exploring.

Your iPhone is a gateway to a world of entertainment and leisure, offering endless possibilities to enjoy your free time. Whether you're immersing yourself in a good book, listening to your favorite symphony, or pursuing a hobby, your iPhone enriches your leisure activities with convenience and variety. Take time to explore and experiment with different apps and services to find what brings you joy and relaxation.

10

Keeping Your iPhone Secure and Up-to-Date

Ensuring your iPhone is secure and up-to-date is crucial for protecting your personal information and getting the most out of your device's capabilities. This chapter covers backing up your data with iCloud and keeping your iPhone's software updated.

Backing Up Your iPhone with iCloud

Backing up your iPhone ensures your data is preserved and can be restored in case of device loss or damage.

- **Setting Up iCloud Backup:** Go to Settings > [your name] > iCloud > iCloud Backup. Make sure iCloud Backup is turned on. Your iPhone will automatically back up to iCloud when connected to Wi-Fi and charging.
- **Performing a Manual Backup:** To manually back up, ensure you're connected to Wi-Fi, then go to Settings > [your name] > iCloud > iCloud Backup and tap "Back Up Now."

Performing Software Updates

Keeping your iPhone's software up-to-date is essential for security and to access new features.

- **Checking for Updates:** Go to Settings > General > Software Update. Your iPhone will check for available updates.
- **Updating Your iPhone:** If an update is available, you'll see an option to "Download and Install." Tap it, and enter your passcode if prompted. Your iPhone will download the update and restart to complete the installation.
- **Automatic Updates:** To enable automatic updates, go to Settings > General > Software Update > Customize Automatic Updates and turn on "Download iOS Updates" and "Install iOS Updates."

Maintaining the security and functionality of your iPhone is an ongoing process, but it doesn't have to be complicated. By regularly backing up your iPhone, and staying on top of software updates, you're taking important steps to protect your device and your personal information. These practices not only keep your iPhone secure but also ensure you have access to the latest features and improvements.

11

Solving Common Problems

Even with the most user-friendly devices, you might occasionally encounter issues. This chapter provides simple steps for troubleshooting common problems on your iPhone, including how to restart your device, force quit unresponsive apps, and when to seek help from Apple Support.

Restarting Your iPhone

Restarting your iPhone can resolve many minor issues, such as an app freezing, slow performance, or connectivity problems.

- **How to Restart:** Press and hold the side button and either volume button until two sliding buttons appear. Slide the one that says "slide to power off" to the right. After your iPhone shuts down, wait a few seconds, then press and hold the side button again until the Apple logo appears.
- **When to Restart:** Consider restarting your iPhone if it's not performing as expected if an app isn't working correctly, or if you're experiencing other minor glitches.

Force Quitting Apps

If an app is frozen or unresponsive, you can force quit it without affecting the rest of your iPhone's operation.

- **How to Force Quit:** On iPhones with Face ID, swipe up from the bottom of the screen and pause in the middle. On iPhones with a Home button, quickly double-click the Home button. This will show all your recently used apps. Swipe right or left to find the app you want to quit, then swipe up on the app's preview to close it.
- **When to Force Quit:** Use this method if an app is not responding to taps or seems to be causing a problem. Remember, force quitting an app should be a last resort, as it can cause you to lose unsaved data in the app.

Seeking Help from Apple Support

If you encounter a problem that you can't resolve through restarting or force-quitting apps, it might be time to seek help from Apple Support.

- **How to Contact Apple Support:** You can reach Apple Support through their website, by phone, or by visiting an Apple Store. For online support, visit support.apple.com to find troubleshooting guides, and contact options, and to schedule appointments.
- **When to Contact Apple Support:** Seek help if you're facing issues that affect your iPhone's basic functions, if your device won't turn on, if you suspect a hardware problem, or if you're experiencing persistent software issues that aren't resolved through restarting.

Troubleshooting common problems on your iPhone doesn't have to be daunting. By following these simple steps, you can resolve many issues on your own. Remember, restarting your iPhone and force quitting apps can fix many minor issues, but don't hesitate to contact Apple Support for more complex problems. Their experts are there to help ensure your iPhone experience is as smooth and enjoyable as possible.

12

Conclusion

C ongratulations on taking this important step towards becoming more familiar with your iPhone! We've covered a lot of ground, from the basics of setting up and navigating your device to using apps, managing communications, enjoying entertainment, and maintaining your iPhone's security and performance.

Here's a quick recap and some words of encouragement as you continue to explore:

Recap of Main Points

- **Getting Started:** We began by introducing you to your iPhone, highlighting key features and basic navigation gestures.
- **Communication:** You learned how to make calls, send messages, and use FaceTime to stay connected with loved ones.
- **Apps and Entertainment:** We explored how to find and use apps for various needs and interests and how to enjoy music, books, and news
- **Security and Updates:** The importance of keeping your iPhone secure and up-to-date was emphasized, along with troubleshooting

common problems.

Remember, mastering your iPhone is a journey, not a destination. It's perfectly normal for learning to take time and practice. Each day, try to explore a new feature or app. Don't worry about making mistakes; they're just part of the learning process.

Your iPhone is a powerful tool that can enhance your daily life in countless ways. Whether it's capturing memories, staying in touch with family, or enjoying your favorite hobbies, your iPhone is there to support you. So, take your time, be patient with yourself, and enjoy the journey. There's a whole world of possibilities waiting for you to explore. Happy exploring!

I hope you found "iPhone for Seniors 2024" both informative and empowering as you navigate your iPhone. Your feedback is invaluable to me and to others who are considering this guide. If you have a moment, please consider leaving a review of this book. Your insights not only help me enhance future editions but also guide others in their journey to becoming more confident iPhone users. Thank you for your support and for being part of our reader community!

13

References

Vognild, A. (2023, October 11). The handy iPhone cheat Sheet for seniors - Sonida Senior Living. *Sonida Senior Living*. https://www.sonidaseniorliving.com/iphone-cheat-sheet-for-seniors/

IPhone User Guide. (n.d.). Apple Support. https://support.apple.com/guide/iphone/welcome/ios

A Getting Started Tour of your iPhone | Senior Tech Club. (n.d.). https://seniortechclub.com/tech-recipe/a-getting-started-tour-of-your-iphone/

www.ingramcontent.com/pod-product-compliance
Lightning Source LLC
LaVergne TN
LVHW051752050326
832903LV00029B/2861